Citizenship Basics 100 Questions Pre Test

Take this 10 question pre-test to see if you are ready for the Civics portion of the United States Naturalization Interview. Remember, you need a *minimum of 6 correct answers to pass:*

1. *What territory did the United States buy from France in 1803?*
2. *What does the President's Cabinet do?*
3. *Under our Constitution, some powers belong to the federal government. What is one power of the federal government?*
4. *What is one thing Benjamin Franklin is famous for?*
5. *The idea of self-government is in the first three words of the Constitution. What are these words?*
6. *Name one U.S. territory.*
7. *We elect a U.S. Senator for how many years?*
8. *There were 13 original states. Name three.*
9. *Who is one of your state's U.S. Senators now?*
10. *There are four amendments to the Constitution about who can vote. Describe one of them.*

Now check your answers. How did you do?

1. *What territory did the United States buy from France in 1803?*

   ▪ **the Louisiana Territory**

   ▪ **Louisiana**

2. *What does the President's Cabinet do?*

   advises the President

3. *Under our Constitution, some powers belong to the federal government. What is one power of the federal government?*

   ▪ **to print money**

   ▪ **to declare war**

   ▪ **to create an army**

   ▪ **to make treaties**

4. *What is one thing Benjamin Franklin is famous for?*

   ▪ **U.S. diplomat**

   ▪ **oldest member of the Constitutional Convention**

   ▪ **first Postmaster General of the United States**

   ▪ **writer of "Poor Richard's Almanac"**

   ▪ **started the first free libraries**

5. *The idea of self-government is in the first three words of the Constitution. What are these words?*

   ▪ **We the People**

6. *Name one U.S. territory.*

   ▪ **Puerto Rico**

   ▪ **U.S. Virgin Islands**

   ▪ **American Samoa**

   ▪ **Northern Mariana Islands**

   ▪ **Guam**

7. *We elect a U.S. Senator for how many years?*

   ▪ **six (6)**

8. *There were 13 original states. Name three.*

- **New Hampshire**
- **Massachusetts**
- **Rhode Island**
- **Connecticut**
- **New York**
- **New Jersey**
- **Pennsylvania**
- **Delaware**
- **Maryland**
- **Virginia**
- **North Carolina**
- **South Carolina**
- **Georgia**

9. *Who is one of your state's U.S. Senators now?*
   - **Answers will vary. Go to http://www.senate.gov/states/# and click on your state**
10. *There are four amendments to the Constitution about who can vote. Describe one of them.*
    - **Citizens eighteen (18) and older (can vote).**
    - **You don't have to pay (a poll tax) to vote.**

Any citizen can vote. (Women and men can vote.)
A male citizen of any race (can vote).

9-10 correct = *You are ready! Take the test now! You do not need Citizenship Basics 100 Questions!*
6-8 correct = *You are probably ready but you should keep studying just in case. Get this book!*
4-5 correct = *You need to study. Get this book!*
1-4 correct = *Definitely not ready for the real thing. You need to study a lot! Get this book!*
0 correct = *Get Citizenship Basics 100 Questions! Study, Study, and then Study some more!*

How to Use Citizenship Basics 100 Questions

The latest research shows that the best way to do well on a test is by **actually taking the test,** several times. This book is formatted for optimal learning by breaking the test questions into **groups of 5 questions**:

- The first set of 5, without questions
- Followed by the same 5 questions, but with the answers.

Read the five questions with no answers and think about what the correct answer is to each question. Then, read the questions again with the answers to check what you got right or wrong. Then continue on to the next set of 5 questions.

This book also has **5 progress quizzes** to see how you are doing as you go through the book. There is **a short, 5 question-quiz after every 20 questions**. If you score 3 or more questions right, then you can feel confident that you are retaining what you are reading. If you get below 3 correct, then you definitely should review that section.

How to Use Citizenship Basics 100 Questions

Spaced Repetition: This book is designed with the scientifically proven "**spaced repetition**" technique in mind. You can learn more effectively when you intensely practice something for a period of time, then take a break, and then review and practice again. This book is specifically laid out for you to do this kind of repeated practice in **doable, 5 question chunks.**

Test Yourself: The latest learning research has also shown that by continually testing yourself, you prepare more effectively for the actual test that you want to take. This book does exactly that by pre-testing you and then giving you 5 progress tests throughout the study book to make sure you stay on track with your studying.

Immediate Feedback: After you read the 5 questions without answers you will then see the same five questions, but this time with the answers. This way you will know immediately whether or not you are retaining the information.

How Citizenship Basics 100 Questions looks inside

5 Questions - No Answers

1. What is the supreme law of the land?

2. What does the Constitution do?

3. The idea of self-government is in the first three words of the Constitution. What are these words?

4. What is an amendment?

5. What do we call the first ten amendments to the Constitution?

5 Questions - With Answers

1. What is the supreme law of the land?

- **the Constitution**

2. What does the Constitution do?

- **sets up the government**
- **defines the government**
- **protects basic rights of Americans**

3. The idea of self-government is in the first three words of the Constitution. What are these words?

- **We the People**

4. What is an amendment?

- **a change (to the Constitution)**
- **an addition (to the Constitution)**

5. What do we call the first ten amendments to the Constitution?

The United States Naturalization Test

To become a naturalized U.S. citizen, you must pass the naturalization test. At your naturalization interview, you will be required to answer questions about your application and background. You will also take an English and civics test unless you qualify for an exemption or waiver. If you don't pass then you will be given two opportunities to take the English and civics tests and to answer all questions relating to your naturalization application in English. If you fail any of the tests at your initial interview, you will be retested on the portion of the test that you failed (English or civics) between 60 and 90 days from the date of your initial interview. ***This study book only concerns the 100 Civics Questions portion.*** For the Civics Portion of the Test:
A naturalization applicant must demonstrate a knowledge and understanding of the fundamentals of the history, the principles, and the form of government of the United States.
To sufficiently demonstrate knowledge of civics, the applicant must answer correctly at least six of ten questions from the standardized civics test form administered by an officer. The officer administers the test orally. Once the applicant answers six of the ten questions correctly, the officer stops the test.

The United States Naturalization Test

Passing the test:

An applicant passes the civics test if he or she provides a correct answer or provides an alternative phrasing of the correct answer for **six of the ten** questions.

Failing the test:

An applicant fails the civics test if he or she provides an incorrect answer or fails to respond to six out of the ten questions from the standardized test form.

Special Consideration - Questions with an *

A USCIS officer gives special consideration to an applicant who is 65 years of age or older and who has been living in the United States for periods totaling at least 20 years subsequent to a lawful admission for permanent residence.The age and time requirements must be met at the time of filing the naturalization application. An officer only asks questions from the three "65/20" test forms when administering the civics test to such applicants. The test forms only contain 20 specially designated civics questions from the usual list of 100 questions. These are the questions that have an asterisk *.

If an applicant fails any portion of the English test, the civics test, or all tests during the initial naturalization examination, USCIS will reschedule the applicant to appear for a second examination between 60 and 90 days after the first examination.

Don't worry, if you study consistently up until your first interview, you should not have a problem.

Finding the Answers to "*Answers Will Vary*" Questions

There are **4** questions on the civics test that have answers that will vary depending on where you live, what state you live in, and what zip code you live in within your state.

20. Who is one of your state's U.S. Senators now?
23. Name your U.S. Representative.
43. Who is the Governor of your state now?
44. What is the capital of your state?

Here are the links to the official websites so that you can find the correct answers to your particular location of residence.

Your state's U.S. Senators:
http://www.senate.gov/states/#

Your state's U.S. Representative:
http://www.house.gov/representatives/find/

Your state's Governor:
https://www.usa.gov/state-governor

Your state's capital:
http://www.50states.com

About the Authors

Darin French

Darin has taught U.S. History, Government, Basic Language Arts, ESL and ESL/Citizenship for the Los Angeles Unified School District since 2007. He has also served as a CBET coordinator, ESL teacher advisor, and participated on several textbook selection committees and WASC accreditation teams. He received his BA in History and Political Science from the University of California at Los Angeles.

Robert Proctor

Robert received his degree from the University of California at Santa Barbara and has been teaching children and adults for over 20 years. He has been with LAUSD since 1996 as an ESL instructor, reading instructor, and teacher advisor. He has worked on numerous textbook review committees as well as presented at many ESL conferences. Robert has co-authored several educational products, including Citizenship Basics.

ISBN - 978-0-615-95815-6

Southern California Educational Services, LLC
4555 E. 3rd St #3B
Los Angeles, CA 90022

Also Available from This Seller:
English Basics: Your Guide to Prepositions

ISBN - 978-0-692-30509-6

Available at:
www.sceduserv.com
or
www.amazon.com

Civics (History and Government) Questions for the Naturalization Test

The 100 civics (history and government) questions and answers for the naturalization test are listed below.

AMERICAN GOVERNMENT

A: Principles of American Democracy

1-5 Questions - No Answers

1. What is the supreme law of the land?

2. What does the Constitution do?

3. The idea of self-government is in the first three words of the Constitution. What are these words?

4. What is an amendment?

5. What do we call the first ten amendments to the Constitution?

1-5 Questions - With Answers

1. What is the supreme law of the land?

- **the Constitution**

2. What does the Constitution do?

- **sets up the government**
- **defines the government**
- **protects basic rights of Americans**

3. The idea of self-government is in the first three words of the Constitution. What are these words?

- **We the People**

4. What is an amendment?

- **a change (to the Constitution)**
- **an addition (to the Constitution)**

5. What do we call the first ten amendments to the Constitution?

- **the Bill of Rights**

6-10 Questions - No Answers

*6. What is one right or freedom from the First Amendment?**

7. How many amendments does the Constitution have?

8. What did the Declaration of Independence do?

9. What are two rights in the Declaration of Independence?

10. What is freedom of religion?

6-10 Questions - With Answers

*6. What is one right or freedom from the First Amendment?**

- **speech**
- **religion**
- **assembly**
- **press**

petition the government

7. How many amendments does the Constitution have?

- **twenty-seven (27)**

8. What did the Declaration of Independence do?

- **announced our independence (from Great Britain)**
- **declared our independence (from Great Britain)**
- **said that the United States is free (from Great Britain)**

9. What are two rights in the Declaration of Independence?

- **life**
- **liberty**
- **pursuit of happiness**

10. What is freedom of religion?

- **You can practice any religion, or not practice a religion.**

11-15 Questions - No Answers

*11. What is the economic system in the United States?**

12. What is the "rule of law"?

B: System of Government

*13. Name one branch or part of the government.**

14. What stops one branch of government from becoming too powerful?

15. Who is in charge of the executive branch?

11-15 Questions - With Answers

*11. What is the economic system in the United States?**

- **capitalist economy**
- **market economy**

12. What is the "rule of law"?

- **Everyone must follow the law.**
- **Leaders must obey the law.**
- **Government must obey the law.**
- **No one is above the law.**

B: System of Government

*13. Name one branch or part of the government.**

- **Congress**
- **legislative**
- **President**
- **executive**
- **the courts**
- **judicial**

14. What stops one branch of government from becoming too powerful?

- **checks and balances**
- **separation of powers**

15. Who is in charge of the executive branch?

- **the President**

16-20 Questions - No Answers

16. Who makes federal laws?

*17. What are the two parts of the U.S. Congress?**

18. How many U.S. Senators are there?

19. We elect a U.S. Senator for how many years?

*20. Who is one of your state's U.S. Senators now?**

16-20 Questions - With Answers

16. Who makes federal laws?

- **Congress**
- **Senate and House (of Representatives)**
- **(U.S. or national) legislature**

*17. What are the two parts of the U.S. Congress?**

- **the Senate and House (of Representatives)**

18. How many U.S. Senators are there?

- **one hundred (100)**

19. We elect a U.S. Senator for how many years?

- **six (6)**

*20. Who is one of your state's U.S. Senators now?**

- **Answers will vary. [District of Columbia residents and residents of U.S. territories should answer that D.C. (or the territory where the applicant lives) has no U.S. Senators.]**

Check Your Progress

Quiz on Questions 1- 20

1. What are the two parts of the U.S. Congress?
2. What stops one branch of government from becoming too powerful?
3. What is the economic system in the United States?
4. What did the Declaration of Independence do?
5. What does the Constitution do?

Go back and check your answers. How did you do? Did you get at least 3 out of 5 correct? OK, good job!

21-25 Questions - No Answers

21. The House of Representatives has how many voting members?

22. We elect a U.S. Representative for how many years?

23. Name your U.S. Representative.

24. Who does a U.S. Senator represent?

25. Why do some states have more Representatives than other states?

21-25 Questions - With Answers

21. The House of Representatives has how many voting members?

- **four hundred thirty-five (435)**

22. We elect a U.S. Representative for how many years?

- **two (2)**

23. Name your U.S. Representative.

- **Answers will vary. [Residents of territories with nonvoting Delegates or Resident Commissioners may**

provide the name of that Delegate or Commissioner. Also acceptable is any statement that the territory has no (voting) Representatives in Congress.]

24. Who does a U.S. Senator represent?

- **all people of the state**

25. Why do some states have more Representatives than other states?

- **(because of) the state's population**
- **(because) they have more people**
- **(because) some states have more people**

26-30 Questions - No Answers

26. We elect a President for how many years?

*27. In what month do we vote for President?**

*28. What is the name of the President of the United States now?**

29. What is the name of the Vice President of the United States now?

30. If the President can no longer serve, who becomes President?

26-30 Questions - With Answers

26. We elect a President for how many years?

- **four (4)**

*27. In what month do we vote for President?**

November

28. What is the name of the President of the United States now?*

- **Donald Trump**
- **Trump**

29. What is the name of the Vice President of the United States now?

- **Michael Pence**
- **Mike Pence**
- **Pence**

30. If the President can no longer serve, who becomes President?

- **the Vice President**

31-35 Questions - No Answers

31. If both the President and the Vice President can no longer serve, who becomes President?

32. Who is the Commander in Chief of the military?

33. Who signs bills to become laws?

34. Who vetoes bills?

35. What does the President's Cabinet do?

31-35 Questions - With Answers

31. If both the President and the Vice President can no longer serve, who becomes President?

- **the Speaker of the House**

32. Who is the Commander in Chief of the military?

- **the President**

33. Who signs bills to become laws?

■ the President

34. Who vetoes bills?

■ the President

35. What does the President's Cabinet do?

advises the President

36-40 Questions - No Answers

36. What are two Cabinet-level positions?

37. What does the judicial branch do?

38. What is the highest court in the United States?

39. How many justices are on the Supreme Court?

40. Who is the Chief Justice of the United States now?

36-40 Questions - With Answers

36. What are two Cabinet-level positions?

- **Secretary of Agriculture**
- **Secretary of Commerce**
- **Secretary of Defense**
- **Secretary of Education**
- **Secretary of Energy**
- **Secretary of Health and Human Services**
- **Secretary of Homeland Security**
- **Secretary of Housing and Urban Development**
- **Secretary of the Interior**
- **Secretary of Labor**
- **Secretary of State**
- **Secretary of Transportation**
- **Secretary of the Treasury**
- **Secretary of Veterans Affairs**
- **Attorney General**
- **Vice President**

37. What does the judicial branch do?

- **reviews laws**
- **explains laws**
- **resolves disputes (disagreements)**
- **decides if a law goes against the Constitution**

38. What is the highest court in the United States?

- **the Supreme Court**

39. How many justices are on the Supreme Court?

- **nine (9)**

40. Who is the Chief Justice of the United States now?

John Roberts (John G. Roberts, Jr.)

Check Your Progress

Quiz on Questions 21-40

1. Who signs bills to become laws?
2. Who does a U.S. Senator represent?
3. What is the name of the President of the United States now?
4. The House of Representatives has how many voting members?
5. How many justices are on the Supreme Court?

Go back and check your answers. How did you do? Did you get at least 3 out of 5 correct? OK, good job!

41-45 Questions - No Answers

41. Under our Constitution, some powers belong to the federal government. What is one power of the federal government?

42. Under our Constitution, some powers belong to the states. What is one power of the states?

43. Who is the Governor of your state now?

*44. What is the capital of your state?**

41-45 Questions - With Answers

41. Under our Constitution, some powers belong to the federal government. What is one power of the federal government?

- **to print money**
- **to declare war**
- **to create an army**
- **to make treaties**

42. Under our Constitution, some powers belong to the states. What is one power of the states?

- **provide schooling and education**
- **provide protection (police)**
- **provide safety (fire departments)**
- **give a driver's license**
- **approve zoning and land use**

43. Who is the Governor of your state now?

- **Answers will vary. [District of Columbia residents should answer that D.C. does not have a Governor.]**

*44. What is the capital of your state?**

- **Answers will vary. [District of Columbia residents should answer that D.C. is not a state and does not have a capital. Residents of U.S. territories should name the capital of the territory.]**

*45. What are the two major political parties in the United States?**

- **Democratic and Republican**

46-50 Questions - No Answers

46. What is the political party of the President now?

47. What is the name of the Speaker of the House of Representatives now?

C: Rights and Responsibilities

48. There are four amendments to the Constitution about who can vote. Describe one of them.

*49. What is one responsibility that is only for United States citizens?**

50. Name one right only for United States citizens.

46-50 Questions - With Answers

46. What is the political party of the President now?

Republican (Party)

47. What is the name of the Speaker of the House of Representatives now?

- **Paul Ryan**

48. There are four amendments to the Constitution about who can vote. Describe one of them.

- **Citizens eighteen (18) and older (can vote).**
- **You don't have to pay (a poll tax) to vote.**
- **Any citizen can vote. (Women and men can vote.)**
- **A male citizen of any race (can vote).**

*49. What is one responsibility that is only for United States citizens?**

- **serve on a jury**
- **vote in a federal election**

50. Name one right only for United States citizens.

- **vote in a federal election**
- **run for federal office**

51-55 Questions - No Answers

51. What are two rights of everyone living in the United States?

52. What do we show loyalty to when we say the Pledge of Allegiance?

53. What is one promise you make when you become a United States citizen?

*54. How old do citizens have to be to vote for President?**

55. What are two ways that Americans can participate in their democracy?

51-55 Questions - With Answers

51. What are two rights of everyone living in the United States?

- **freedom of expression**
- **freedom of speech**
- **freedom of assembly**
- **freedom to petition the government**
- **freedom of worship**
- **the right to bear arms**

52. What do we show loyalty to when we say the Pledge of Allegiance?

- **the United States**
- **the flag**

53. What is one promise you make when you become a United States citizen?

- **give up loyalty to other countries**
- **defend the Constitution and laws of the United States**
- **obey the laws of the United States**
- **serve in the U.S. military (if needed)**
- **serve (do important work for) the nation (if needed)**
- **be loyal to the United States**

*54. How old do citizens have to be to vote for President?**

- **eighteen (18) and older**

55. What are two ways that Americans can participate in their democracy?

- **vote**
- **join a political party**
- **help with a campaign**
- **join a civic group**
- **join a community group**
- **give an elected official your opinion on an issue**

▪ call Senators and Representatives
▪ publicly support or oppose an issue or policy
▪ run for office
write to a newspaper

56-60 Questions - No Answers

*56. When is the last day you can send in federal income tax forms?**

57. When must all men register for the Selective Service?

AMERICAN HISTORY
A: Colonial Period and Independence

58. What is one reason colonists came to America?

59. Who lived in America before the Europeans arrived?

60. What group of people was taken to America and sold as slaves?

*56. When is the last day you can send in federal income tax forms?**

- **April 15**

57. When must all men register for the Selective Service?

- **at age eighteen (18)**
- **between eighteen (18) and twenty-six (26)**

AMERICAN HISTORY

A: Colonial Period and Independence

58. What is one reason colonists came to America?

- **freedom**
- **political liberty**
- **religious freedom**
- **economic opportunity**
- **practice their religion**
- **escape persecution**

59. Who lived in America before the Europeans arrived?

- **American Indians**
- **Native Americans**

60. What group of people was taken to America and sold as slaves?

- **Africans**

people from Africa

Check Your Progress

Quiz on Questions 41-60

1. When must all men register for the Selective Service?
2. Who lived in America before the Europeans arrived?
3. Name one right only for United States citizens.
4. Who is the Governor of your state now?
5. What is one reason colonists came to America?

Go back and check your answers. How did you do? Did you get at least 3 out of 5 correct? OK, good job!

61-65 Questions - No Answers

61. Why did the colonists fight the British?

62. Who wrote the Declaration of Independence?

63. When was the Declaration of Independence adopted?

64. There were 13 original states. Name three.

65. What happened at the Constitutional Convention?

61-65 Questions - With Answers

61. Why did the colonists fight the British?

- **because of high taxes (taxation without representation)**
- **because the British army stayed in their houses (boarding, quartering)**
- **because they didn't have self-government**

62. Who wrote the Declaration of Independence?

- **(Thomas) Jefferson**

63. When was the Declaration of Independence adopted?

▪ July 4, 1776

64. There were 13 original states. Name three.

▪ New Hampshire
▪ Massachusetts
▪ Rhode Island
▪ Connecticut
▪ New York
▪ New Jersey
▪ Pennsylvania
▪ Delaware
▪ Maryland
▪ Virginia
▪ North Carolina
▪ South Carolina
▪ Georgia

65. What happened at the Constitutional Convention?

▪ The Constitution was written. The Founding Fathers wrote the Constitution.

66-70 Questions - No Answers

66. When was the Constitution written?

67. The Federalist Papers supported the passage of the U.S. Constitution. Name one of the writers.

68. What is one thing Benjamin Franklin is famous for?

69. Who is the "Father of Our Country"?

*70. Who was the first President?**

66-70 Questions - With Answers

66. When was the Constitution written?

- **1787**

67. The Federalist Papers supported the passage of the U.S. Constitution. Name one of the writers.

- **(James) Madison**
- **(Alexander) Hamilton**
- **(John) Jay**
- **Publius**

68. What is one thing Benjamin Franklin is famous for?

- **U.S. diplomat**
- **oldest member of the Constitutional Convention**
- **first Postmaster General of the United States**
- **writer of "Poor Richard's Almanac"**
- **started the first free libraries**

69. Who is the "Father of Our Country"?

- **(George) Washington**

*70. Who was the first President?**

(George) Washington

71-75 Questions - No Answers

B: 1800s

71. What territory did the United States buy from France in 1803?

72. Name one war fought by the United States in the 1800s.

73. Name the U.S. war between the North and the South.

74. Name one problem that led to the Civil War.

*75. What was one important thing that Abraham Lincoln did?**

71. What territory did the United States buy from France in 1803?

- **the Louisiana Territory**
- **Louisiana**

72. Name one war fought by the United States in the 1800s.

- **War of 1812**
- **Mexican-American War**
- **Civil War**
- **Spanish-American War**

73. Name the U.S. war between the North and the South.

- **the Civil War**
- **the War between the States**

74. Name one problem that led to the Civil War.

- **slavery**
- **economic reasons**
- **states' rights**

*75. What was one important thing that Abraham Lincoln did?**

- **freed the slaves (Emancipation Proclamation)**
- **saved (or preserved) the Union**
- **led the United States during the Civil War**

76-80 Questions - No Answers

76. What did the Emancipation Proclamation do?

77. What did Susan B. Anthony do?

C: Recent American History and Other Important Historical Information

*78. Name one war fought by the United States in the 1900s.**

79. Who was President during World War I?

80. Who was President during the Great Depression and World War II?

76-80 Questions - With Answers

76. What did the Emancipation Proclamation do?

- **freed the slaves**
- **freed slaves in the Confederacy**
- **freed slaves in the Confederate states**
- **freed slaves in most Southern states**

77. What did Susan B. Anthony do?

- **fought for women's rights**
- **fought for civil rights**

C: Recent American History and Other Important Historical Information

*78. Name one war fought by the United States in the 1900s.**

- **World War I**
- **World War II**
- **Korean War**
- **Vietnam War**
- **(Persian) Gulf War**

79. Who was President during World War I?

- **(Woodrow) Wilson**

80. Who was President during the Great Depression and World War II?

- **(Franklin) Roosevelt**

Check Your Progress

Quiz on Questions 61-80

1. What happened at the Constitutional Convention?
2. What did the Emancipation Proclamation do?
3. Name one problem that led to the Civil War.
4. Who was President during World War I?
5. There were 13 original states. Name three.

Go back and check your answers. How did you do? Did you get at least 3 out of 5 correct? OK, good job!

81-85 Questions - No Answers

81. Who did the United States fight in World War II?

82. Before he was President, Eisenhower was a general. What war was he in?

83. During the Cold War, what was the main concern of the United States?

84. What movement tried to end racial discrimination?

*85. What did Martin Luther King, Jr. do?**

81-85 Questions - With Answers

81. Who did the United States fight in World War II?

- **Japan, Germany, and Italy**

82. Before he was President, Eisenhower was a general. What war was he in?

- **World War II**

83. During the Cold War, what was the main concern of the United States?

- **Communism**

84. What movement tried to end racial discrimination?

- **civil rights (movement)**

*85. What did Martin Luther King, Jr. do?**

- **fought for civil rights**
- **worked for equality for all Americans**

86-90 Questions - No Answers

86. What major event happened on September 11, 2001, in the United States?

87. Name one American Indian tribe in the United States.

INTEGRATED CIVICS

A: Geography

88. Name one of the two longest rivers in the United States.

89. What ocean is on the West Coast of the United States?

90. What ocean is on the East Coast of the United States?

86-90 Questions - With Answers

86. What major event happened on September 11, 2001, in the United States?

- **Terrorists attacked the United States.**

87. Name one American Indian tribe in the United States.
[USCIS Officers will be supplied with a list of federally recognized American Indian tribes.]

- **Cherokee**
- **Navajo**
- **Sioux**
- **Chippewa**
- **Choctaw**
- **Pueblo**
- **Apache**
- **Iroquois**
- **Creek**
- **Blackfeet**
- **Seminole**

- **Cheyenne**
- **Arawak**
- **Shawnee**
- **Mohegan**
- **Huron**
- **Oneida**
- **Lakota**
- **Crow**
- **Teton**
- **Hopi**
- **Inuit**

INTEGRATED CIVICS

A: Geography

88. Name one of the two longest rivers in the United States.

- **Missouri (River)**
- **Mississippi (River)**

89. What ocean is on the West Coast of the United States?

- **Pacific (Ocean)**

90. What ocean is on the East Coast of the United States?

- **Atlantic (Ocean)**

91-95 Questions - No Answers

91. Name one U.S. territory.

92. Name one state that borders Canada.

93. Name one state that borders Mexico.

*94. What is the capital of the United States?**

*95. Where is the Statue of Liberty?**

91-95 Questions - With Answers

91. Name one U.S. territory.

- **Puerto Rico**
- **U.S. Virgin Islands**
- **American Samoa**
- **Northern Mariana Islands**
- **Guam**

92. Name one state that borders Canada.

- **Maine**
- **New Hampshire**
- **Vermont**

- **New York**
- **Pennsylvania**
- **Ohio**
- **Michigan**
- **Minnesota**
- **North Dakota**

Montana

Idaho

- **Washington**
- **Alaska**

93. Name one state that borders Mexico.

- **California**
- **Arizona**
- **New Mexico**
- **Texas**

*94. What is the capital of the United States?**

- **Washington, D.C.**

*95. Where is the Statue of Liberty?**

- **New York (Harbor)**
- **Liberty Island**

[Also acceptable are New Jersey, near New York City, and on the Hudson (River).]

96-100 Questions - No Answers

B: Symbols

96. Why does the flag have 13 stripes?

*97. Why does the flag have 50 stars?**

98. What is the name of the national anthem?

C: Holidays

*99. When do we celebrate Independence Day?**

100. Name two national U.S. holidays.

96-100 Questions - With Answers

B: Symbols

96. Why does the flag have 13 stripes?

- **because there were 13 original colonies**
- **because the stripes represent the original colonies**

*97. Why does the flag have 50 stars?**

- **because there is one star for each state**

- **because each star represents a state**
- **because there are 50 states**

98. What is the name of the national anthem?

- **The Star-Spangled Banner**

C: Holidays

*99. When do we celebrate Independence Day?**

- **July 4**

100. Name two national U.S. holidays.

- **New Year's Day**
- **Martin Luther King, Jr. Day**
- **Presidents' Day**
- **Memorial Day**
- **Independence Day**
- **Labor Day**
- **Columbus Day**
- **Veterans Day**
- **Thanksgiving**
- **Christmas**

Check Your Progress
FINAL Quiz on Questions 81-100

1. Name two national U.S. holidays.
2. Where is the Statue of Liberty?
3. What is the name of the national anthem?
4. Name one state that borders Canada.
5. Why does the flag have 50 stars?
6. What is the capital of the United States?
7. Name one of the two longest rivers in the United States.
8. What ocean is on the East Coast of the United States?
9. What major event happened on September 11, 2001, in the United States?
10. Name one American Indian tribe in the United States.

Go back and check your answers. How did you do? Did you get at least 6 out of 10 correct? OK, good job! Now you should be ready for your citizenship test! If you don't feel confident, then go back and do it again. GOOD LUCK!

** If you are 65 years old or older and have been a legal permanent resident of the United States for 20 or more years, you may study just the questions that have been marked with an asterisk.*

Made in the USA
Middletown, DE
02 May 2017